T0118103

THE SEA CABINET

Caitríona O'Reilly was born Dublin in 1973, grew up in Wicklow and Dublin, and now lives in Lincoln. She studied archaeology and English at Trinity College Dublin, and later held the Harper-Wood Studentship in English Literature from St John's College, Cambridge. Her first collection *The Nowhere Birds* (Bloodaxe Books, 2001) was shortlisted for the Forward Prize for Best First Collection, and won the Rooney Prize for Irish Literature. Her second collection, *The Sea Cabinet* (Bloodaxe Books, 2006), was a Poetry Book Society Recommendation and was shortlisted for the *Irish Times* Poetry Now Award in 2007. Her third collection, *Geis* (Bloodaxe Books, UK; Wake Forest University Press, USA, 2015), won the *Irish Times* Poetry Now Award 2016, was shortlisted for the Pigott Poetry Prize in association with Listowel Writers' Week, and was a Poetry Book Society Recommendation. She is a freelance writer and critic, has written for BBC Radio 4, translated from the Galician of María do Cebreiro, and published some fiction. She has collaborated with artist Isabel Nolan, edited several issues of *Poetry Ireland Review*, and was a contributing editor of the Irish poetry journal *Metre*.

CAITRÍONA O'REILLY

The
Sea Cabinet

BLOODAXE BOOKS

ISBN: 978 1 85224 705 8

First published 2006 by
Bloodaxe Books Ltd,
Eastburn,
South Park,
Hexham,
Northumberland NE46 1BS.

www.bloodaxebooks.com
For further information about Bloodaxe titles
please visit our website and join our mailing list
or write to the above address for a catalogue

Supported using public funding by
ARTS COUNCIL
ENGLAND

Digital reprint of the 2006 Bloodaxe Books edition.

For Ted Hickey

1940-2005

ACKNOWLEDGEMENTS

Acknowledgements are due to the editors of the following publications in which some of these poems first appeared: *Agenda, The Bend, Èire-Ireland, Grand Street, The Irish Times, Poetry Ireland Review, Poetry Review, The Stinging Fly* and *The Times Literary Supplement*; *Modern Women Poets*, ed. Deryn Rees-Jones (Bloodaxe Books, 2005), *The New Irish Poets*, ed. Selina Guinness (Bloodaxe Books, 2004) and *The Wake Forest Irish Poetry Series*, vol.1, ed. Jefferson Holdridge (Wake Forest University Press, 2005); and *Three-Legged Dog* (Wild Honey Press, 2003).

'The Sea Cabinet' was broadcast on BBC Radio 4 in March 2003. 'A Quartet for the Falcon' formed part of an exhibition mounted during the Humber Mouth Literature Festival in 2003.

Caitríona O'Reilly gratefully acknowledges a Society of Authors grant in 2005.

CONTENTS

13   Poliomyelitis

14   Lag

15   Gravitations

17   Persona

18   The Maze

20   X-ray

21   Diffraction

23   Floater

24   Duets

25   To the Muse

27   Hierophant

28   A Qing Dish

29   Netsuke

31   Shortcut to Northwind

34   In the Deaf Man's House

34   I *Who are these coming to the sacrifice?*

34   II *Yo lo vi*

34   III *The Sleep of Reason*

35   IV *Sabbath-Asmodeus*

35   V *Palimpsest*

36   Six Landscapes

36   I *The River*

37   II *Littoral*

39   III *Uggool*

40   IV *The Avenues*

41   V *On Beverley Common*

42   VI *In Aragón*

43   A Deserted House

44   The Sea Cabinet

44   I *The Ship*

46   II *The Mermaid*

47   III *The Esquimaux*

49   IV *The Unicorn*

50   V *The Whale*

52 But to the Girdle do the Gods Inherit

53 Stalker

54 A equals B. B equals C

56 Bempton Cliffs

57 A Quartet for the Falcon

57   I *The Mews*

59   II *Opus Contra Naturam*

60   III *The Lure*

61   IV *The Curée*

62 Now or When

63 Calculus

64 Heliotrope

66 Electrical Storm

68 Pollen

69 An Ending

70 Envoi

...and when we proceed further, and consider that the mystical cosmetic that produces every one of her [Nature's] hues, the great principle of light, for ever remains white or colorless in itself, and if operating without medium upon matter, would touch all objects, even tulips and roses, with its own blank tinge – pondering all this, the palsied universe lies before us a leper; and like wilful travellers in Lapland, who refuse to wear colored and coloring glasses upon their eyes, so the wretched infidel gazes himself blind at the monumental white shroud that wraps all the prospect around him. And of all these things the Albino whale was the symbol.

HERMAN MELVILLE, *Moby-Dick*

Poliomyelitis

The pool at the centre of the broken-tiled room
was once a swimming pool for local boys

with boils on the neck and chilblained knees.
Their old joints murmur like the sea's

gradual encroachment on the choked-up
gorge of nineteen-fifties *noblesse oblige*:

grass sprouts from the rafters of the Big House
now, like hairs from a pensioner's nose.

The swimming pool was long ago condemned
though a rusty ladder still dissolves at one end

and even the gulls won't land on water
this brackish and rancid. I carry the taint of it

away like my father, bend over it in dreams
to watch the dead plants thrive beneath the water,

the pocked silt open and the nymphs rising
to invade another element, breaking the surface

till the room's air fills with black butterflies
brushing their wings against my mind's ceiling.

Lag

Although it is the hottest day of the heatwave, clouds
are hauling their sackcloth bellies over volcanoes,
        leaving silvery animal
        or mineral traces behind.

The liquid will never seep far enough down
to kill that angry flicker in the earth's throat.
        Seams of live fire
        like snakes or veins are feeling

the surface. The extinct naturalist with his primitive camera
could tell the whole story with his burnt bones,
        only they do not speak.
        And this is what I wake up in –

mornings where it rains and I have forgotten my name.
What lapses from an eye not quick enough to see
        ivy hooking itself to a tree,
        how the numb foliage explodes?

Gravitations

March: the grey atom
I've swallowed drops,
element-heavy plumb line

to this year's mood –
as mercury might smash
its instrument –

drops through vapours,
humours, that acrid
snarl of the gut that,

stretched, would circle
the house, the city,
the planet on which

my feet stood,
when last I looked.
I am six months

nearer the earth.
I have barely moved
all winter.

Faces pass
as though their owners
went on wheels.

And still it drops
stopless, niagaric –
is it the principle

of gravity in me –
that waking
is falling, lying still

is falling?

Persona

The mud-brown river is clotted with débris.
And what can I do with these dark adhesions,
These unmoored pieces of the night?
They breathe their black into my day –

What can I do with these dark adhesions?
If dreams are rooms in which my self accretes,
They also breathe their black into my day.
As a mannikin, I set myself to work

In dreams or rooms in which my self accretes.
See me there with the pained carved face.
As a mannikin, I've set myself to work
Until the lost loved one appears

And sees me there with the pained, carved face.
I cannot get these wooden limbs to work
Until the lost loved one appears
To shrink at the slyness of my puppet-smile.

I cannot get these wooden limbs to work.
Nothing is different from nothing, I say,
And shrink at the slyness of my puppet's smile.
Chrysanthemum dragons shimmer in the room

But nothing is different from nothing, I say,
These unmoored pieces of the night,
These chrysanthemum dragons shimmer in the room –
Still the mud-brown river is clotted with débris.

The Maze

I live in a space that was bequeathed me,
a ziggurat of stepped spires and corridors.
      There is no road out.
Mornings, solar rays puncture the spiral,
and the unsheathed cornea shrinks
      like a snail at an object –

the corners, the slanted ends on everything.
There is an itch, and sometimes,
      among the whorls
of the breast's adhesive coral, a filament of blood.
What rises at this is the sound of the maze,
      a red noise that pounds

through aortic roads and storm-drains
in which, like caves, I have tried to hide.
      Nights are the worst,
spent under the thin grey blanket, listening
to the shifting rumours issue through the routes of the maze,
      waiting for what rises.

There are no words in the maze, no signs
pointing a way through the puzzle that daily distends,
      infecting mountains and fields
and all the city's membranes. And like a city,
what was loved and entered, or ignored
      dilapidates, an eyesore.

Inside these wincing walls, things are not
what they seem. I must be more watchful
      for what rises
within a lidless dark that never splits,
as I pass again through its twisted routes,
      mislaid perspectives.

I never remember the road,
though I take it nightly. Each night
    the light lessens.
Each night new pathways open to terminate
like shut valves or lopped thoracic branches,
    nowhere.

X-ray

A vertical chain of spine:
flesh cloaks the bones'
articulation in shadow.
The Tree of Life, but not
of Knowledge: shot through
with this god's radiance, light
shook from his metallic hair,
the gravity of his glance
decreeing me unscrolled
as the killer might decipher
his victim, delicately
parting the belly's vellum.
I am lain against the plate
and dazzled: the light inimical,
the weight that enters weightless.
A thrown shadow dissects
the self from what it was.
Can flesh become all shadow?
Not yet: as through a glass
brightly and fragile as a bird's
shine my long blue bones.

Diffraction

Œil qui gardes en toi
Tant de sommeil sous un voile de flamme...
PAUL VALÉRY

The electrical cicadas,
the little brown lizards,
here on the hill

light's own properties
colour the landscape in.
Those rocks on which

the theatre perches
are from the Greek:
sand-gold sea bullion,

and in the high cemetery
the cenotaphs' duty
is to face an impossible blue.

I stumble among them
in the heat-struck noon,
seeking a tomb

by the lavender beds.
The sun-striated sea.
The thousand gazing sails

of the dead.
And the light –
it fills my eye-vessels

to overflowing, shifting
the rods and cones
of their ravenous geometry.

Not the Catalan woods,
their calm green, their
shy beasts out of Rousseau,

can rub from my sight
this dazzle.
Days later I notice it –

a half-moon gone,
half a sentence
smudged from the page.

It was the dark
ajar in my head,
a portion so aswarm

with ants or flies
it was invisible.
At St Pau hospital,

its medical machinery
buried in earth,
I am seen inside.

Argus, my x-ray, says:
there are limits to what
any eye can absorb.

Floater

Just lying here in the angled
sunlight, watching the leaves
shadow-stipple my window,
it suddenly swims into sight
like a snaggle-toothed sea-beast

submerged until now,
jellied eel in my vitreous humour.
It could be a crayon-scrawl
high on the wall were it not
for those snake-tongue darts

and feints it makes as my eye flicks,
frantic to catch itself up.
What vandal took a house key
to the windscreen? I dangle it
in space like a puppet,

watching it creakily shift
its nodes and joints. Caduceus –
telluric snake on a stick,
casting off the dull cells
from its refractive coat –

littering the bottom of my eye
with its pile of minus signs,
its nest of hair, a worm-cast
or caddis-case from which
(invisibly) some brisk beast fled.

Duets

Underneath, her voice is
a whalebone-and-cambric
arrangement, a set of stiff stays

or pegs, well-hammered-in.
She is a house with firm foundations.
Her fabric pulls apart

in the upper floors only,
where something can be heard
fluttering with calculated frailty,

a coquette's attenuated eyelash
or lace-fringed can-can dress,
a spinning coin dropped

on a polished table,
an ornamental dove trapped
in an attic, beating tired wings.

Her voice has entered every corner of itself.
The boy's voice is an arrow pointing upwards.
Its flute-notes issue from an instrument

still half a sapling, with green feet in the ground
and a flicker of leaves around its crown.
It has the gothic hollowness

of cathedral pipes, a cylindrical sound,
which is the shape a boy's voice makes
crossing its own vast space.

To the Muse

Are we condemned to repeat, you and I,
the scenario of the railway station tea-room,

like the river that perpetually grazes its heels
against the castle battlements, our encounters

always ending where they start?
At Kilkenny the confederacy faltered.

Our one-way conversation was like milking
a mastitic cow who regards you

reproachfully, her face framed by caesarean
kiss-curls the shape of question marks.

There was sexual failure in the guesthouse bedroom,
a broken shower and a groaning cistern,

which we were too far gone to welcome
as Romantic squalor. As I watched my pupils

vacillate in the bathroom mirror, troubled
by the proximity of asymmetry to a cemetery,

you kicked your heels in St Canice's churchyard,
(its corpses nourished on dung

from Cromwell's chargers) the picture of chagrin,
observing the phallic tilt of the bell tower,

the Elizabethan lady's tuning fork head-gear.
Meanwhile all I could think about at the castle,

under the purple ash toppled by last week's storm,
was my trip here aged eleven, the hung-over

driver glowering on the school bus,
whose indecent advances the evening before

brought the masonry of childhood definitively tumbling,
confirming even my worst imaginings.

Hierophant

It was the oldest, coldest place in England:
his face emerged as from a dark pool
that night, the indifferent calm eyes deep,
a reticence in the bridge of the nose, hands
white as cuttle-bones. As though I'd drunk
the winter sun from the fen, pale and cool
as the sea-shell curve of his lip, I sank
like a silver hoard beneath him in sleep.

A Qing Dish

Qianlong the stone-grinder stands to work at his trestle table.
His veins are paining. For years he has been grinding one piece of jade:
a white river boulder from the cold streams of Yarkand, in the West,
where wading river-girls find stones that flush to the temperature of blood
at the touch of their numb footsoles and water-wrinkled hands.
What a skin it had…until the knife, loaded with toad-grease
and powdered almandine, bit deep enough to reveal an interior
of the most precious kind: the white of mutton-fat, clear and rare.

Qianlong is no sculptor. He can exhaust the jade only
with harder stones, with garnet, crushed emery or chips of ruby,
can only persuade it into patterns fit for an emperor's gaze.
He frowns. Behind him the wide plains are filled with ancestors' bones,
some disarranged in graves robbed of their stones, some in repose,
their tongue jades falling slowly through the osseous hoops of their jaws.
Although he ignores the constellations spinning above him,
the Mongol winds that shape the hills circling his Yellow River home,

Qianlong knows something of all these. He is a kind of scholar.
He knows the bi disks, jade astrolabes, not for the heavens
(the stars have migrated like cranes since then) but for the serpents
surfacing on the jade's rivery skin. These he has learned,
with the sacred tiger, the cicada, the tinkling walls of Song vases.
He understands the lust of the fingers for small gems, beads
and amulets, the lips' desire to wear the stone thin with kissing.
His wife is worrisome. Lü Ta-Lin, his pupil, gives her lotus flowers.

Qianlong gives her jade combs for her hair. His assistants gather.
Now he mixes fine diamond dust into the grease and smears it
on the leathered end of his bamboo stick. Quickly, before the sun brushes
the tips of the hills, Qianlong props his dish beside the window.
It is circular like the sun, its bevelled edges revealing, as petals,
a base in which two waxy catfish swim in and out of *lingzhi* scrolls.
When the sun declines, the dish is fired with a watery glaze like celadon,
like light through ice or mist or paper, or the rarest of all whites, nephrite.

Netsuke

I walk on thin soles
this dense season.

No wind lifts the leaves,
the thickened stream

shakes no reeds.
I spread my fan,

hide half my wan
face, pale with lead,

pale with the shit
of nightingales.

The marks they limn
on my nape

might have been
knife marks,

stark when I blushed
at his figurines:

women and men coiled
round each other

like worms,
a tongue-cut sparrow,

a nest of rats.
They keep his objects

from sliding down
that long silk cord

he hangs beside
his genitals, and being

lost. When I draw
his blade across my

arm it resembles
water dripping over

a stone lip
in the stone garden,

runny wax
from a candle,

the new moon's
incised smile.

Shortcut to Northwind

I opened it expecting something else –
the icon *Shortcut to Northwind* on a borrowed machine –
but found nothing but a white glare from an empty screen.
And after all, what was it I had wanted,
if not some afterthought of his on which I'd counted?
Its regular flicker was an electrical pulse

that made the thick glass undulate.
It reminded me of falling back on sheets,
cool sheets, with him that day in June –
at least the falling movement seemed the same,
but it was a desert I entered. What heights
those rock-needles reached I couldn't speculate.

And it was dark there though I seemed to see
by moonlight – it was moonless – a mica-glitter
or schist-shine from the wasteland all around me.
Then the wind picked up. Desert winds are bitter,
murdering with stones too small to see
that have ground each other down for centuries

and will for centuries to come. The red breath
of the desert screeched its grievance in my face
in a devil- or a lion-voice. It said:
there are worse things than the silence of the dead.
The silence that the living keep, that is a voice
of stone that will condemn. Condemn to Death –

and then it snatched me upright off my feet
and took me to a space awash with light
like diamonds thinly sprinkled on the night
or seeds sown in the furrows of darkness.
Did someone hold my hand? The air's thickness
grew, and it was without fright

I knew that I was breathing water.
It was like sliding down the surface of a jade,
like entering the glossy throats of flowers.
All the while a thin string of bubbles like tears
fell upwards from me. This rope of bead
was all that held me to the surface of the water

as I watched the sea nosing its calcined captives
like a creature, rolling them over in the sand.
A mariner's dead face wore a blue toothy smile
and his blond fronds wavered in the underwater wind.
A galley's nutmeg turned mother-of-pearl
pale in the descending light, all rippled and restive.

I could have rested there. It would have been
a salty sleep on the tongue of a mollusc,
under a nacreous canopy. But something shattered
my watery chandelier and littered
the sea's pavement with spears or narwhal-tusks
or blades of ice as hard as anything I'd seen.

And I was lifted bodily, still dripping wet,
out of the sea and into the chill of the air.
The frigid blast of his breath froze my hair
to waves of ice and froze my fingers and toes
as he wrapped me in his wings and rose
with me into the North. The stars went out

when he trailed his dirty cloak across the hills
and I saw nothing but the icicles in his beard
and eyebrows. In his pupils, back and wide,
a frosty fire burned. And he said
nothing. It was a kind of consummation, hard
and comfortless, it was exchanging one spell

in the desert for another. I dream
now of getting back to my resistless life,
to music like river-water makes in a gourd,
those plunging harmonies, myself a leaf
drunk on the surface tension and singing aloud.
Not staring at this blank and empty screen.

In the Deaf Man's House

I *Who are these coming to the sacrifice?*

The town spews forth its varlets
this morning like black bile.
This view suffices me for windows.
I know the noble citizens by sight:
I have made them articulate
like a snake that clings
to the sexual outline of the earth,
their clot of moaning faces as its head,
their mouths issueless as flowers
opening on walls of silence.

II *Yo lo vi*

The matadors minced in their
coats of light, the forms of women
glowed like moons in my youth.
Now in this bitumen-flicker
I see prognathous Jane, old rot-nose
cavorting with devils in her sleep,
sucking the penis of a billy goat,
or vomiting prophetic eggs.
I have seen it: anything may happen
between these dark disordered walls.

III *The Sleep of Reason*

My friend, you write about the cold
and how the words themselves
seem cancerous. On these walls
faces take the place of words.

I have heard nothing for many years
but the animal-breath of madness
in my ear. The open skies
smite me with imaginary noise.
I keep to my house, conjuring
inquisitors from cracked plaster.

IV *Sabbath-Asmodeus*

I cannot hear my own footfalls,
so like a sad sleeper kicking
a foot free from twisted sheets,
I am condemned to dream.
Am I the one that Asmodea
smothers in her red cloak?
That town on the anvil-shaped hill
withstands the light's assaults.
Prodigiously sick and dizzy
I fall nightly over its edge.

V *Palimpsest*

My original scheme foresaw
a *fête galante* of supine duchesses,
majos done in daubs of flesh and silks.
Instead I watched the python Time
devour them all and tore myself to bits
below the unoffending sky.
Then I learned the uselessness
of light. These walls absolve me
of the years' thick impasto,
of the scrawl that became my life.

Six Landscapes

I *The River*

The coming night breathes an atmosphere
of childhood October in crisp light and wood-smoke,
    and the guy ropes
    sway in the harbour
while the black river pauses
    between two tides,
    shaping itself in shadow.

It is never changing, never the same –
the ancient trees of the rookery in silent commune
    with the river's
    different darkness
when we pass, and this time,
    an egg-speckled kestrel
    bullied by swallows.

A field that was mysteriously full of nothing
once but poisoned sparrows, a convulsive rain,
    is brown earth now,
    would not disturb
the bubble in a spirit level,
    with a manhole like
    a navel at its middle.

We wonder how will the river change, escape
development, or work its careless necromancy
    on the next ones
    to come here –
and who will watch its black dreams
    shatter into figments
    skulled and crossboned in light?

II *Littoral*

By the campsite, travellers'
greyhounds lick the junk they find
and sniff along a wall sprayed

RELEASE IRA PRISONERS
and further on, HANG THEM ALL.
I pass a line of bollards

stuck with blue stones off the beach
like pins on a pin-cushion.
The theme is blue, or slate-grey

maybe, like the tame sea is –
its stones seem banded with blue
like pillows, mollified by

the sucked-in breath of the sea.
Its creamy exhalations
leave them quite unmoved, just bruised

darker by the toppling tide.
I stare, in a slate-grey mood,
pretending nothing's realer

than the colour of the beach-
stones' blueness. Which is less like
blue the further down you go.

I select seven of them,
seven stones totalling home:
a dark one scored with crazy

yellow strokes like fossil grass
or hopscotch on a pavement,
a flat one like a mountain-

ridge in outline, capped with snow,
one like a mesolithic
axe-head, but more beautiful,

smooth basalt flecked with sequins,
one crossed with mineral lines,
one rock ringed like a planet,

one riddled with reddish specks
the texture of crayon wax.
An ostrich-egg of granite.

III *Uggool*
(for Seán and Jessica Lysaght)

It was only when the road ended
and the engine stopped ticking
that we noticed the silence
that was of space unfolding
and ourselves absorbed by it,
unburdened by the light's extension.

Seen from the hill, Clare Island
hung between identical elements,
neither air nor ocean, and a list
of islands ran to the curve of the world.
I recognised the feeling:
we brought the weight of us to leave

at the rim of a perfect water,
or our idea of it, not the peat stream
underneath the senile thorn tree,
but this strand with its kelp straps
and shell-scourings, that furnace-boom
along the country's vanquished edge.

Any other year I would have watched
across the bay and seen the fold of a horizon,
the weather move south. Here, it catches
me asleep. The gleam of new snow

enters my room like the sound of a horn
on the fog-bound Humber. Strange that in a place
of so much sky there is just one view,
but it is England, and to each his own portion:

between the cracks on my neighbour's frozen pond
and the saffron throats in my crocus garden
there is no relation. Daily, the brownish stain
from the tannery chimney smudges the sky

to which the black bare trees are lungs.
I keep my side of the bargain, tamping
down the tulip bulbs, uprooting the weeds
in my walled half-acre, letting the cat in

as the kitchen windows glow at five o'clock
and human noises seep between the hedges.
Down the darkening cinder-path, fenced at both ends,
their children's voices cry to me like owls.

V *On Beverley Common*

Here is unfenced existence
PHILIP LARKIN

The minster's gold stones
tell of a settled polity
the minstrels on the walls
sing and fiddle
fiddle and sing
to the yeomanry
their mouths agape
their music now reaching
those nearer stars
and at the town's edge
this draped landscape
pasture rising to meet
the sky and someone's
herd wandering where
Clare might have sat
and not wept at fences
elephant limbs of the elm
flowers whose names
we have forgotten
and the thorn tree's
mezzotint trunk
plates in a closed storybook
the chestnut drops a lime
spatulate leaf where
the silence waits
                    O presences
and in the green cathedral
birds pipe from the eaves
the fox's topaz eye
hesitates.

VI *In Aragón*

Caspe – a parched sigh
the earth emits at midday

when the sun's reign heightens
over hills of yellow or pale orange dirt,

studded with agave harsh enough
to have and keep its liquid core.

Seventy years since,
this earth quenched itself

to some forgotten end
(any arid cone could be another);

the Ebro holds itself still inside
its dark blue dream, and the trees

twist with the effort of rising.
In Caspe, light pours through the gap

the hills create in being at odds
with each other against the flaming sky,

and shows their horizontal faces
grooved and inscrutable in the Spanish way

and as indifferent to the force that shapes them,
giving them fractured hearts for their fractured bones.

A Deserted House

What but design of darkness to appal?

It was the noise in the chimney that reminded me of it, less a buzzing than that deep boom the sea makes in a cavern, the noise of an underground process, a concussion.

I thought of the bee colonies in the mansion house chimney. In the absence of fires set by roughened hands, in that sulphurous and cobwebby shaft, pierced by a rod of light each noon, the waxen cells are painstakingly constructed.

It is the tiredest of metaphors, this six-sided suburb, but what perturbs us now is the logic of its order, like something our production-line minds might concoct, one grub to each cell invariably, incarcerated hatchlings.

Day on day the noise of industry grows in the chimney, afflicting the whole house with tinnitus.

Still the dust motes drift through the curtained rooms, Cupid on his pedestal smiles slyly through his scarf of transparent marble, and as usual no wicks are lit in the Fascinating Lamp Room.

There is just a noise like the sea gnawing at the distant edge of England, gaining a yard or so each year. What made him go, the Seigneur of Holderness, who was steadfast through religious trouble, who understood the meaning of wars?

He vanished, leaving his vintage cellar and ouija board, his riding crop on the hall table. He vanished, and the skeletal whale outside the ha-ha fell to pieces, jangling its mammoth bones.

In the chimney of his house the noise grows. The bees will continue to build, varnishing their hexagons with propolis for the city's defence. Who now, on hearing that rumour, would infer: *less a haunted house than a population in the chimney piece?*

43

The Sea Cabinet

(in the Town Docks Museum, Hull)

> *Sideways hurled*
> *This krang o' a warld*
> *The sun has flensed*
> *Is lyin' forenenst*
> > HUGH MacDIARMID,
> > 'Krang'

> *There is a Leviathanic museum, they tell me, in Hull, England.*
> > HERMAN MELVILLE,
> > *Moby-Dick*

I *The Ship*

Below the just-set sun and the Polar stars
a mist appears and scrolls about the graves
that stand like canted yards of anchored fleets
or tumble home, their forms declined and bitten now
with lichen to the bone. Horns on the Humber
sound no longer for John Gravill (his bones here lie)
captain of the world's first steam-driven whaler
the *Diana*, whose death resulted from *exposure, anxiety,*
and shortness of provisions during a four-months
imprisonment in the ice, surrounded by all
the dreariness and perils of a cold and desolate
arctic winter. She halted home months later,
his chilly corpse tarpaulin-wrapped on the fo'c'sle.
A panel on his grave depicts the ship,
cruelly beset, aslant inside the giant squeeze of ice.
How many nights did her scurvy crew lie,
possessions tied in gaskets by the bed,
hearing the hull shriek like a diphtheric child in sleep,
waiting for the shout of the watch? She was not crushed
like her Dundee sister Princess Charlotte,
whose crew returned to blast the splintered hulk,
extract whisky like ambergris from a whale's belly,
and hold a drunken revel on the ice.

                                        Theirs is a world
enclosed in ice, a rime that forms like salt
corroding Captain Gravill's name, old porthole glass
with its rippling distortions. In the empty museum
in Queen Victoria Square, a whaling-boat protrudes
as though from a half-thawed iceberg overhead,
affording a whale's-eye view of its sharpened harpoon
of dark soft iron, with stop-withers like a fish-hook's beard
for lodging deep in blubber, only to be hacked clear.
It is spanned on ready for the chase, and seven hundred
fathom's worth of line lies coiled like worsted in the boat.
A stuck whale is a fast fish, and dives so quick
a pigging pail must quench the fire the friction starts.
Elsewhere the flensing tools keep an iron repose,
spotlit but obscure, ruminating in their dark way
on the tendency of tools to outlast their forgers, their users,
and even the monsters whose bulk they divided.
They hang on the walls, looking as though they might fall
from revenge or neglect, black and contorted as an alphabet:
whale lances, flensing spades, blubber knives
and tongue knives, blubber pricks and seal picks,
trypots and pewter worms, gaffs and staffs and bone gear,
oil funnels, loggerheads, kilderkins and runlets,
spurs for clambering up the slippery sides of whales;
the whaleman's glossolalia and horizon.

Between the imaginary iceberg and the skeletal whale
is the stuffed and mounted mermaid in her case,
the crudely-stitched seam between skin and scale

so unlike Herbert Draper's siren dreams, loose
on the swelling tide, part virgin and part harpy.
Her post-mortem hair and her terrible face

look more like P.T. Barnum's Freak of Feejee,
piscene and wordless, trapped in the net of a stare.
She has the head and shrivelled tits of a monkey,

the green glass eyes of a porcelain doll, a pair
of praying-mantis hands, and fishy lips
open to reveal her sea-cave mouth, her rare

ivory mermaid-teeth. Children breathe and rap
on the glass to make her move. In her fixity
she's as far as can be from the selkie who slips

her wet pelt on the beaches of Orkney
and walks as a woman, pupils widened in light,
discarding the stuffed sack of her body.

Without hearing, or touch, or taste, or smell, or sight
she echoes the numb roll of the whale
in a sea congealed with cold, when it was thought

no beast could be as nerveless as the whale.

III *The Esquimaux*

The two Esquimaux or Yacks,
Male and Female, brought home
by Captain Parker, of the ship
Truelove, of Hull, from Nyatlick,
in the Cumberland Straits,
on the West side of Davis straits,
WILL BE EXHIBITED
on Thursday and Friday,
March 9th and 10th,
in the Lecture Hall, York,
for two days only, previous to their
return to their Native Country
on the 20th Instant.
This interesting married couple,
Memiadluk and Uckaluk,
(whose respective ages are seventeen
and fifteen) are the only inhabitants
ever brought to England
from the Western Coast.
They will appear in their Native Costume,
with their Canoe, Hut, Bows and Arrows etc.

Their plaster heads keep company in the cabinet,
as if to witness that home is a relative term.
His lower lip's flatness, the sombre planes
of his skull's gradual dome
show a resolute teenager's warrior calm,

but his pretty young wife Uckaluk
grimaces when the smothering whiteness covers
her babyish face. Amazingly salty tears
are squeezed from tight-shut eyes until it is over.
Her upset look suggests it is not over.

The good ladies of Hull shudder lightly inside
their baleen martingales and whalebone stays
as Memiadluk, the flesh-eating Esquimaux,
hoists his bow and arrow and strikes a pose
suggestive of savagely innocent ways.

Uckaluk is taught the rudiments of household
economy, the proper care of glassware, china
and knives, and how to braise a leg of beef
(of great practical use in the tundra).
Both profess themselves covered with honour

to encounter Greenland Man, the Esquimaux effigy
with his stitched paddle and sealskin boat
fashioned by a distant forebear. He sits stiffly
in the next cabinet, surrounded by fishing-floats
and hinged seal toys, and a delicate

harpoon foreshaft, carved from the pizzle bone
of a whale. And Memiadluk and Uckaluk
keep their eyes closed on a future in which
she dies on board ship of measles only weeks
from home. Memiadluk went back alone.

IV *The Unicorn*

A most excellent drink made with a true Unicorn's horn, which doth effec-
tually cure these diseases: Scurvy, Old Ulcers, Dropsie, Running Gout,
Consumptions, Distillations, Coughs, Palpitation of the Heart, Fainting
Fits, King's Evil, Rickets in Children, Melancholy or Sadness, the Green
Sickness, Obstructions, and all distempers proceeding from a Cold Cause.
   The use of it is so profitable, that it prevents diseases and infections, by
fortifying the Noble Parts, and powerfully expels what is an enemy to
Nature, preserving the Vigour, Youth, and Good Complexion to Old Age:
the Virtue is of such force, as to resist an Injury from an Unfound
Bedfellow, none can excel this, for it is joined with the Virtue of a true
Unicorn's horn, through which the drink passeth, and being impregnated
therewith, it doth wonderfully Corroborate and Cure, drinking it warm at
any time of the day, about a Quarter of a pint at a time, the oftener the
better, the Price is 2s the Quart.

The true Unicorn is not the white horse of legend,
coaxed by the droplets staining a virgin's blue bodice,
but the corpse-pale Narwhal, with its counter-clockwise swirl
of jousting tooth, heraldic as any animal.
Ground, it could vanquish poison, and in goblets or spoons
rinsed the provender of crowned and syphilitic heads.
That the bulbous asymmetry of its otherwise
toothless skull should culminate in such a twisted myth!
Armies of Narwhal congregate, like Rhinoceri
at their sub-Saharan drinking holes, fencing to breathe,
and are pulled by their noses onto the ice. Tokens
of love for the sweethearts of Hull whalers, walking canes
and bedsteads, these are the Unicorn's final blazon.

V *The Whale*

The twenty-ninth letter of the Arabic alphabet
is *nun*, which means 'a whale'. 'A fall, a fall'

is what the Arctic whalers called, meaning
'a whale'. God rested the Earth on an angel's

shoulders, the angel on a rock, the rock on a bull,
and the bull on the back of a whale. Beneath

is water, air, and darkness of a kind that laps
about these cabinets of scrimshawed teeth,

morse-tusk and baleen, while giant jawbone
yat-steeads stand as far away as Hereford,

as though a whale had fallen from the clouds,
scattering blanched bones. The Humber bridge

yawns like the Right whale's sieve of vertical
Venetian blind, the bowhead's snappy crop of umber.

The next room tells the scientific story
of the Mysteceti, now mythic as a unicorn.

Wall-maps chart migrations they once made,
while on a loop, their disembodied voices cry

within a range that can be heard. Belugas,
whales white enough to terrify Ishmael, sing

from their spouts, even with chimneys ablaze.
Whalers called them Sea Canaries, sending them

down into darkness, extracting the oil
to light their age from the sea's deep chambers.

It is they who are in darkness now.
The whale on which their world depended

is elsewhere, free of history, and casts
their antique lives adrift like ambergris.

But to the Girdle do the Gods Inherit

It's true we are the stuff of nightmare,
peopling the caves of your dreams,
at one with the pewter fog and sea.
We rise as the sea releases, disinterred
from the kist-graves of your mind's
fifth layer of destruction. Imagine
how it is with us: our stone implements,
our combs and early mirrors, ceding
no reflection. Even to ourselves unknown.
Whether the salt-sting of our indivisible
lower halves is pain, or akin to pain,
we cannot say. Yet we shine.
Prisoners of your regard, it is the glitter
of sea that beguiles you, the cold grey
irises of her many dead. Pictures
of a death forever out of reach,
with our famished nightmare mouths.

Stalker

Eyeing my own nakedness in a broken mirror
as the red-coloured money changed hands,
I woke to a sound lighter than wind in dry grass
and listened again, marooned on the near side of sleep
with prickling palms. I turned on the light.
A spider on the wooden beam over my bed

resumed its wavering walk. I'd sensed the rasp
of legs like brittle fingernails in sleep,
that bunched torso hung from its knuckles,
so I hit it once and watched it drop,
legs curled in reflex to the shape of a net,
as if snaring itself in its own quick death.

A equals B. B equals C.

We are getting
from A to B.
We are getting from A

to B in our shellacked
capsule, accompanied
by this arterial hum,

this song of tedium.
Heat of grief –
the kind that tears

purport to cool
but never do –
hot as the place

from which they come,
and come. There is no
space left between

the broken white lines
for anything now
but outbreaks –

the fox's out-of-nature
stillness by the road,
our imagination of its

ruined eye, its famous
white snout. Also
these cousin-casualties –

hare dead in the dust,
keeping the secrets
of its broken oval head.

We are getting from
A to B. Reflected trees
flow over the windscreen

and from the eyes inside
water tries to fall
like something natural.

Bempton Cliffs

The blank-faced gun emplacements
　　　　stare out to sea.
Nothing's changed since the war.
　　　　It is land for the grasshopper
and lark, then suddenly air
　　　　and the sea's sharp glance.
The first time we almost missed them,
　　　　the wind carried
away their voices, that football-roar
　　　　from the terraces.
Then an updraft like a wave's explosion
　　　　brought guano-stink,
and with it rumours of a high-rise civilisation:
　　　　so garrulous, so peeping-busy.
Down where the sea heaves
　　　　like the quilt of a restless sleeper,
the feeders are. Industry will not cease
　　　　for questioning – the heating seas,
the sand-eels' migration –
　　　　but fewer each year
from their chalky sockets
　　　　those swart eyes stare.

A Quartet for the Falcon

I *The Mews*

My falcon is snatched from the air.
It is the dark time. I have cast
sweet-smelling rushes on the floor
and the walls are unlimed.

I keep a lamp burning in here.
Outside, England dreams under
a mantle of legendary snow,
her trees stood bare, aghast,

her spine stiffened against winter.
History is yet to happen.
I have banished the tercel-gentle
beyond hearing, while my lady

waits her change.
I have hidden her creance and bells
sounding their chord of freedom;
her buttercup feet keep the perch.

Twenty nights I waked her, haggard,
till she flew to the lure and stooped in air
to dive into my flittered dreams,
fixing them with her stares and ways.

Now I have seeled her eyes again,
hiding their black beams
with a stitch to each golden underlid,
knotting the threads behind.

She cannot see the spider twitch
on the rafter, nor the lamp's slow flicker.
She is blind to her own change
as all men are but I, witnessing

The colours drop from her breast,
the mineral glint of her back
go shabby as the waned moon
under a tonneweight of shed feathers.

II *Opus Contra Naturam*

I feed her decoction of diamond-skinned adder,
hawker's prophylaxis, proof against taint in the wing.
That she should absorb the snake's cunning
makes me her alchemist, rattling the atoms
in a vitreous well. Red sulphur, argent vive, even
1,1,1, trichloro-2, 2bis (parachlorophenyl) ethane:
solve et coagula. Behold the work of my hands –
dead metals litter the ground, my poor bird sickens
and will not rise until warmed by a flame to the limbeck.
I have made a sealed world to hatch heavenly birds,
Their flight a cloud-burst, a rain of mercurial feathers,
while outside the peregrine atom wanders
through field, seed and leaf, and through the egg's
chamber: thin-shelled and toxic on the eyrie's edge.

III *The Lure*

Snared in a mode of seeing,
the raptor's eyes unseel again.

Not an outline scarfing the blue wind
but several worlds unscrolling:

the chemical plant's logical conduits
glitter like the keys of a flute

while brown earth casts up
bones of its lost alluvial people:

shards of Delft in a Dutch landscape.
Abandoned churches ride the horizon

like high ships. She is caught in the rigging –
such details as flowers in dark grass,

calligraphic wings imped by a scribe
to *fiat lux*, or mantling their Marian prey.

Over a bleached Segovian plain the eye
seeks its eagle like the sky's pupil.

Aguila, describing a brutal circle.
Slow clouds tumble from the cooling stacks.

Anchor, tear-drop and cut diamond –
now her sentimental silhouette descends

to a swung horseshoe bound in leather.
It is the World, the Flesh, the Devil.

The secretive hart turns at bay,
lowers his tines to the hounds' cry.
The sword enters the bull's heart –
   still he stands,
  amazed on the red sand
as the stony unbeliever might,

who has seen God. Soon now
horns will sound *dedow*
for the unmaking. Beaters flush
   the grey heron
  like a coney from its warren,
the peregrine's jet eyes flash.

They go ringing up the air,
each in its separate spiral stair
to the indigo rim of the skies,
   then descend
  swift as a murderer's hand
with a knife. Death's gesture liquefies

in bringing the priestly heron down.
Her prize, the marrow from a wing-bone
in which she delights, her spurred
   fleur-de-lys tongue
  stained *gold-vermilion* –
little angel in her hangman's hood.

Now or When

On the sundial at Beverley Minster

All of my days fall into this easy measure.
The sun in his ecliptic marks me, as candles
describing lucent circles in the dark. From my
high place on the wall I have seen the down-at-heels
pass in their own cycles, imagining their flesh
cold and perishable as the moon, my other
light. Moss overgrows me, and from my crumbling mouth
mottoes drop implacable as stones. *Nobody*
looks at me when the sun is not there. Is it good
always to say the same thing? My tilt no longer
mirrors the world's, or the calculations have changed.
The last is hidden so we have to watch them all.
Every decade since, his path has been removing,
his meridian eluding me, rooted here
unmoving and unmoved. *O light, I hope for thee*
in this darkness. I pray this earthly pendulum
swings back towards its first innocent embroidery
of stars – *time is an arrow that flieth* – and I
can regain my zenith. *Remember life is short.*

Calculus

Here is the letter I wanted to write, the one
that shows me succumbing to the light's blandishments

like a Vermeer housewife, my silk skirts swollen
as mariposa tulips, my complexion milky.

I collect fine words the way others collect birds' eggs:
for kestrels' I have *roseapple*; for wrens' *pearlwort*.

Were it not that my natural disposition is hurried,
you'd have me convinced the most beautiful word in the language

is *haemostasis*, which means the stopping of clocks,
the scientific observation of what ticks on in an interval

during which I am detained by shadows, those details
(again) you'd have me accrue: the copper moth's clownish flight

in my yard, how the sweet pea tethers itself to those
scalene strings I've pinned to the wall. Each day at noon

I drive another nail in to mark the day's high-water moment,
the sun's clumsy arabesque in that makeshift analemma

I've sketched on the floor: your regard's incalculable angle.

Heliotrope

Past beautiful,
stuck in the dust

of a road, her thin
branched head

with its baby hair
and dozen white eyes

so anthropomorphised
and mute – her lover

going down the sky
daily in his flaming steps

and she with her
padlocked gaze –

eternal follower!
Yet the circle's story

fixes her
at its centre –

her greenish rooted
limbs keep company

with all the buried
girls and boys

whose lost testes
and ovules stir to life

again this month –
under the soft rain

of a god's grief
the hyacinth and lotus

come, with narcissus
on his sex-struck stem.

Electrical Storm

1

And like everything it began with the sea,
that week I spent rinsing myself clean of it,
upheld by its salts, a tracery of venous weeds
round my white ankles. There was nothing
of you in the routes of the sky, those parts
of the horizon I endured. When I arose

it was from a bed: the weight of the sea fell away.
On that night a storm split the sky in two.
Its tearing entered my dream, entered a room
in which we kissed, though I did not know you.
The voice of the storm became your voice,
its lightning, your eyes' most delicate veins.

2

At daybreak the azure was vacant.
Only a morning mist still clung to the pines
and it seemed a day of no consequence
after a dream-time's *sturm und drang*.
But by evening they'd strung the torches
out again, and the wine in our glasses

held the deep glow of their light
and it fell on our faces below the porch,
when we agreed that my country had become
a country of high walls, it fell on your
prismatic face and it scattered over mine,
and the glass shivered in my hands and broke.

3

No horizon could be huge enough to hide
this longing, when like an egg the instant
cracks wide, and what tumbles out
are our days with their easy arrangements.
We are two tired children under such
dishevelled stars. We follow the dark road

to where the company stands under lamps,
but the colour of your eyes is in my marrow.
When our hands touch it is a seeing,
not that blind leaning of plants to the sun,
but the rediscovered memory of how to touch
as our fingers find each other in the dark.

4

Your smile occurs everywhere when it occurs,
its left-over glimmer's in this late summer
weather, in the sheen on the wasp's tiered back,
in those exhausted marks of torsion on the sky.
It leaves me marvelling at my conventional hunger,
though the scales of the sea will settle back on me,

and the leaves drop from a hibernating sky,
and my grey eyes turn colour. Your absence
leaves its stain on the day like those shadows
that leak from the sides of tall buildings,
flow down small streets and mix with the night
in which I can never think of you belonging.

Pollen

Lying with one eye open I can see
a yellow spot staining the clean sheet

I put there yesterday,
a fleck of yolk suspended

in albumen, gold coin at the end
of a barren viscous sea

for those brave enough to stain
their lives to gild the Virgin's mantle.

Their blood mixed with foam
dries to crackling on the shores of Spain.

Azafrán – the colour of evening sun,
the flavour of honey that never reaches

the lips, edging instead a labyrinthine Gospel,
spilling its light inside the borders.

Even now I can barely contemplate
its brightness in the eye of the bee,

how it dusts his muscular back
and grain for grain matches his gold

in the gasp of the calyx,
in the petal's ragged breath.

An Ending

Hay-bales high as totems
in the cold grooved fields,

like blond and stocky giants
glimpsed from the road's

ridge by ridge-unspooling
ribbon. You were doing sixty

when the hare broke
from the hedge, your instinct

to swerve taking us
to the bank's edge, not over.

Such a pair we'd have made,
though, in the smashed Ford:

cameo-style forehead to waxwork
forehead, a slow trickle of liquid

from our mouths' corners, posthumous
bruises dappling our temples.

Tucked up in rumpled metal
as if in bed. There would have been

wreathes, orations.
Hands would have wrung.

Envoi

And although it will be
the same story –
the going out

under violet stars
that seem to pin
your skull to the sky –

you will do it:
bending your ear
to their ravenous desires.

'We realised some time
ago that restlessness
was not to be assuaged' –

so it will challenge
your store of images,
those cheques you draw

against yourself.
Who can say
if a loved face will lie

at the end of it?
Death, desirelessness:
such kinless things.

Printed in the USA
CPSIA information can be obtained
at www.ICGtesting.com
JSHW082226140824
68134JS00015B/745

9 781852 247058